A Stray Dog, Following

Greg Quiery

Stairwell Books

Published by Stairwell Books
161 Lowther Street
York, YO31 7LZ

www.stairwellbooks.co.uk
@stairwellbooks

A Stray Dog, Following © 2020 Greg Quiery and Stairwell Books

All rights reserved. No part of this publication may be reproduced, stored in or introduced into a retrieval system, or transmitted, in any form, or by any means (electronic, mechanical, photocopying, recording, e-book or otherwise) without the prior written permission of the author.

The moral rights of the author have been asserted.

ISBN: 978-1-913432-06-5

Layout design: Alan Gillott
Cover Image: Shanshan0312
Edited by Rose Drew

My thanks to Colin Watts for his most valuable advice, support and comment. Thanks also for the encouragement I have received from Sarah McClelland and all the regulars at the Dead Good Poets, and to Ali and the Liverbards. Thanks to Tanvir Ratul who first published At Kenny. I am very grateful to Rose and Alan at Stairwell for all their work in bringing this to print. And thanks most of all to Kath for her support and understanding.

Table of Contents

Lies	1
Burnt Out	2
At Kenny	3
Warming	5
On Exchange Flags	7
At Cappaghmore	8
Boon Companion	9
Against the Heart	10
'Twas in the Town of Drumlin	11
Paper	13
Cillin	15
One Adventure Yet	17
Departed	18
Ghosts	19
Fred	20
The Belfast Blitz	21
In the Days Before They Left Iar Connaught for Chicago	23
Two Uses for Cowhide	24
Gone to Canada	26
The Rules of War	28
Ramadan	29
Seeds	30
The Fiery Couch	31
Vanished	33
Handkerchief	34
Why Ferry Turf by Boat?	35
Rostrevor	36
Each Time You Kill a Tree	38
Fulmar	39
Grass	40
Zero Emissions	42
Her Chair	43
Down in These Waters	44
Sue	45
Apple Blossom	46
Arenig Fawr	47
Iron Man	48
Snowflake	50

Lies

People eat lies as if they were pure honey
So easily swallowed, they trickle down the throat
To sooth the mind, and warm the chambers of the heart.
People drink deeply of deception,
Eager to quench their thirst for righteous justice with delusion.
Hungry for the proof and rectitude
Of their one true faith.

Lies, faithful dogs, lie submissive at your feet,
Eager to please,
While simple truth remains aloof, unbending.
Lies put on the garments you command,
While humble truth stands naked
Greets you with an honest stare;
Her frank expression shines a light in each dark corner.
Lies hammer out the awkwardness of truth,
Lend the cloak of certainty to deception.
Lies, nurtured in resentful hearts,
Let loose all fears
And bathe them in the sweet release of anger
To wash away the last of doubt in a feverish rush to judgement.

Truth will out they say.
But lies are half way round the world
Before truth ever wakes.
And lies lie gloried in the sun
While truth lies buried in her unmarked grave. //

Burnt Out
During the Troubles, following a shooting, the getaway car would often be driven to a quiet spot and torched.

In the purple light of dusk it crackled
Red and yellow tongues around the tyres
That chariot of fires.
Declaring its own brand of beauty to the dusk
The driver's seat a pit of dying flame
Twitching shadows spitting out sparks
From the roasting paintwork.
The perfect sweep of windscreen glass
Shattered diamonds scattered on the gravel
Crunched beneath our feet.
Bulky puff balls, thick black smoke, billowed up
To stream into the evening air
And drift across the gable wall
Darkening the stern Red Hand of Ulster,
The tang of roasted tarmac and fried rubber
Drifted to the hawthorn hedge
And across the field
To agitate the nostrils of the dozing cattle.

Beyond the car park, council houses turned their backs
Yard doors shut as tight as any butcher's cold room
Determined to be unperturbed,
Knowing to never see or hear.

Later in the night, we drove home
Flat tones from the radio announced – amongst much other news –
A shooting at the Rath estate.

At Kenny

At Kenny all we had was cars thundering past the office window,
Chip papers blowing on the pavement, a leaky roof.
And she would stand out by the car park at the back
Her shallow face the pallor of her thin white cardy
Too short at the sleeves
The lighter poised between her finger and her thumb
The ciggy in her other hand, held well away.
She huddled by the office wall, out of the wind,
Glanced about and shivered
A mouse in search of bolt hole.

She chatted now and then
About how the dog was overweight
And, like her fellah, too big for her flat.
And how he – the dog, that is, not the fellah – wasn't right.
And how he – the fellah, not the dog –
Threw a wobbler when he seen the cost of the injections,
And how she gave the worming tablets to them both
Without letting on.
Such a waste of space, that fellah.
Never condescended to appear at our office parties,
Though we'd see him coming to collect the car keys sometimes,
Slobby, sour-faced, trousers too big at the rear.

They tried for kids
He put the blame on her.
She went for tests,
But we never heard the outcome.
And when she found out what he was up to with that bar-maid
Things got worse
Then her dad turned up,
After all those years when he had never bothered.
Emphysema. Needed her to call by now and then,
Well, most days actually,
On her way home from the office.

And then they found asbestos – in the office, not the dog –
So after all those years
They moved us out of Kenny
To a faceless sixties block
Across the road from Sefton Park
Where she could stand out in the cold
See the grass and trees, and blow smoke to the breeze.

Then the day came when the circus pitched a tent
Across the road, inside the park.
The caravans all along the kerb outside the office.
He was a knife thrower,
In tight black sleeveless t-shirt
Spaded beard. A Harley Davidson tattoo on his fat upper arm,
Looking for a light.
And she with shallow face the pallor of her thin white cardy
Too short at the sleeves
Passed the lighter poised between her finger and her thumb.
And reached to stroke the doggy at his side, a Labrador,
Who used to be a guide dog for the blind, he said
Though he himself could actually see quite well
Being a knife thrower.
She told him all about her dog, her fellah and the worming tablets.
We heard his big laugh all the way up to the office.
The circus packed up on the Sunday.
She never showed on Monday
Or any other day for that matter.
The boss was not best pleased,
Agency staff are such a cost these days.
The dog, of course, had died some months before. ⁄⁄

Warming

The birch is withered in the heat
The swallows come no more in spring
The grass is buried under dust
Where the dry winds sing.

There's a stranger on the road tonight.
A thin silhouette against the flaming sky
Day long we watched him in the shimmering heat
Bleached by a red sun, as he climbed the hill.
And now he goes from door to door along the derelict flats
In search of scraps.

What befell those hundreds,
Who once passed here,
On their passage north,
North to where the bleached bones lie?
Weary ragged mobs, sand in their throats
Eyes dark as mountain pools,
Their rangy horses stacked
With whatever they had salvaged
And that rattling tinkling sound,
Of empty canteens against their ribbed flanks,
Tunics heavy with the smell of wood smoke,
Their minds delirious with the thirst.
All fight gone out of them,
Coming from the south, the fires, the massacres.
Which we no longer hear of, since the signals died.

And now these days
More often just a single one, like this.
We watch what he'll do next, the tall man on his own
Dry as a raisin,
Now with a stray dog following.

With dark comes quiet,
Unbroken even by a siren's call.
We've become accustomed.

And as that solitary man is enveloped in the shadows,
We mount a guard around the well,
Lock the gates,
Release the dogs into the compound.

The birch is withered in the heat
The swallows come no more in spring
The grass is buried under dust
Where the dry winds sing.

On Exchange Flags

Exchange Flags, the square behind Liverpool Town Hall, was an important centre for the conduct of the slave trade. It later became the centre of the international cotton trade. Merchants would hold samples between their fingers, agree a price and then drop the cotton on the ground.

Back in old glory days, long since forgotten,
The flags here were smothered in snowy white cotton.
Soft as a carpet beneath merchant feet
King Cotton was plenty, King Cotton was cheap
It came by the Mersey, it came by the seas
By white canvass aloft in the westering breeze.
By Liverpool sailors, nimble and yar
Tough as mahogany, weathered as tar.

It came from the rivers, it came from the mud
It came from the kick and the stick and the blood
It came from the work line, the whip, the plantations
It came from the fracture and breaking of nations.
For cotton is gentle, fragile and light
Cotton is pure and pristine and white.
But the commerce of cotton, darker than death
Would barter your soul and crush your last breath.

It went by the steam, the engine, the rail
It went by the hundredweight, bail over bail
It went by Manchester, Bury and Preston
Blackburn and Bolton, Darwen and Nelson
There's brass for the boss, and poor spinning Jenny
Works hour by long hour for less than a penny.
Where the dust was so thick it smothered the lung
And thundering looms drowned the Lancashire tongue.

Cotton by boll, by bag and by bale
For smocks and for shirts, for duck cloth and sail.
Cotton for mills, for ships and plantations
For enriching mill owners, impoverishing nations
Cotton for tyranny, hardship and slavery
Cotton for unions, resistance and bravery
Back in the glory days, long since forgotten
It came by the Mersey, that snowy white cotton. //

At Cappaghmore

We took the lonely road for miles and miles
That carries on from no place to nowhere.
Turned into the narrow sunken lane
And pulled up by the hedge.

The dull door thud, the last mechanic sound
Sunk instantly in leaf swell and bee pulse,
Behind a curtain of thick hazel brush we found
The path.

Floored with those grey rounded Burren stones
Cool beneath the whispering canopy
We trusted to its winding route in trees
From no place to nowhere,
As though it cannot seem to make its mind
Careless what direction it should take,
Or how much time expend.
Keeping to the measure of this place.

The first sign was a siskin at a feed
Slung across a clearing on a string.
Then on a snatch of wind a flash of gold
Finches in a bunch.

The cabin was itself close hemmed by hazel
Almost as if sprung from stony earth.
Each detail crafted by one pair of hand's
Steady energy and skill.
Hunkered there, in warmth of wood
Protection from the westering wind
The rain above and cold beneath.
It draws you to that old demanding thought.
All that one man needs is captured here.

Boon Companion
Written on the 100th anniversary of the outbreak of the Great War. 1914 – 1918

Our house is peaceful in the dark,
But in the trenches of the night I wake again
Companion to the dead
As we begin once more this lurid vigil,
His bloodied face before me, imprint on a shroud
He never says a word, nor asks a question
No anger. No recrimination,
Just a burning search to understand.
And those hollows in the head,
Where once were windows to the world, blinded by sacrifice,
Now more serene than those that are alive could ever be.

Why can't he join his comrades in the ground?
Those tangled bones down in the barrows
Each locked into the pose they took when we first heaved them in,
All purpose buried with them in the mud
Beneath the waking world they crouch
Each one with his private crown of thorns,
And lost ambition.

Downstairs I pour a drink. Am I the only one he greets like this?
The vigil of the vacant eyes.
I might command him one last time to 'Go,'
But surely, he has learned by now not to obey.
And besides, who would I have to talk to then?
Not the living, I know that.
I pour four fingers more, and stare into the hollows of my boon companion
There where all the horror lies.
As together we await the dawn.

Against the Heart

Who can craft a swallow's tail but swallows?
Who alone can form the eagle's wings?
Who but a lark can launch the lark's sweet song
High over summer meadows where she sings?

Who can weave the spider's web but spiders
Laced with dew drops glistening in the breeze?
Who can make red admirals but butterflies
And who can grow the forest but the trees?

And though you capture glories of the sun
And though you harness power of the wind
And though you now can move the very mountains
Against the heart of nature you have sinned.

The image of each being you may capture
Every one record and give a name
However much you document each creature
The chainsaw and the plough treat them the same.

Don't they have ears to hear and eyes to see?
Don't they have blood to shed and tears to cry?
All you who wear the cloak of life, know this,
Those who together live, together die.

'Twas in the Town of Drumlin
The idea for this came from a story by Downpatrick writer Lynn Doyle

'Twas in the town of Drumlin, in the County Down
There was a grand big meeting of the farmers all around
Who agreed to work together, to establish a co-op
A better way to get their dairy products to the shop.
The idea was accepted with a show of hands
The unanimous approval of those men who worked the land
With such fraternal feelings, it didn't make no odds,
That half of them were Fenians, and the other half were Prods.

Then up stood big Ned Crilly, said he really had to mention
A matter of importance which had escaped attention.
'When going to the shops, how can housewives take their pick
If they can't tell which milk is Protestant, and which is Catholic.'
The meeting then decided to avoid communal friction
They'd separate the bottles by devotional conviction
On Protestant farm produce red labels would be seen
While on the Catholic milk, of course, the labels would be green.

To you and me this simple rule is absolutely clear
But it wasn't very long before big problems did appear
When Jim McCann, a Catholic, took his cow down to the mart
And sold it to a Protestant by name of Tommy Smart
When Smart got home his wife said, 'Can you tell me now,
How can you make Proddy milk, when you've bought a Catholic cow?'
When told by the Committee, his milk would never pass
Says Smart, 'The cow is Catholic, but it's eating Proddy grass.'

Then Willy Orr, Grand Master of the local Orange Order
Was caught smuggling cheap Catholic hay in across the border
And someone pointed out, that you're taking a quare chance
When the wind blows Roman Catholic rain in from Spain and France
Then to compound the crisis the priest at Ballybilk
Had a lady in confession say she'd drunk some Proddy milk
So he drafted out a letter to the Pope himself in Rome
To get official guidance direct from the papal throne.

The Vatican committee was alarmed at the suggestion
That the flock were in such danger of heretical ingestion
Though drinking Proddy milk itself was not in the extreme
It could lead to Proddy butter, Proddy yoghurt, cheese and cream.
All Catholics should beware the threat of excommunication
When adding milk to tea without papal dispensation.
And Protestants should recognise the risks that they can take
Of betraying God and Ulster when they order their milk shake.

Paper

They say it's best to start with a clean sheet.
So I've returned to paper,
Trustworthy stuff you can take between your fingers
Hold up to the light,
A pristine white rectangle,
Where I can make a fresh beginning.
I've stepped back from the alluring glow,
To take back control
From the cyber-Geist
The gremlins, the machine
The false impressions of being,
Where one stab will conjure up a perfect letter
In whatever font, in such mint condition.
One sleight of hand a word
Each line of words as unblemished as a mouth of Hollywood teeth
Straight-lined, and evenly spaced
Readable, clean, reliable.
Putting us at one remove, me and the word

Why would anyone put that aside
To retrieve the pen,
Gripped awkwardly between finger and thumb,
To make contact with the paper,
And one by one create imperfect shapes?
Drunken chaotic words
Which expose my own unique interpretation
Of the curly twists of alphabet
Allowing anyone in turn to read,
Through my contorted threads,
My impatience, indifference to good order,
Inconsistency,
Exposed by that font first forged in concentration
By hard-pressed fingers and clenched tongue
At my wooden childhood desk,
Where Mr Fairley once used the blackboard
To tell how trees became pages.
Our link to the invention of the ancient cultures.

And how we think of them today
Sheets that can return to earth.
Each one a carbon lock.
I muse on this as I reverse the page,
And run my finger-tips down the back
To feel impressions left there by the pen,
The nobbled spine of the living word.

Cillin

The title refers to the unmarked hidden burial grounds where the bodies of babies, whose souls were deemed by Catholic doctrine to be excluded from heaven, were sometimes interred. Some were those conceived 'out of wedlock', others children who died before being formally baptised.

Whirring and spinning
We came down on the breeze,
Launching out towards the waves
At the far tip of the island.
And under vault of pure blue heaven
Spun again
Down to the tussocks and the tide
Discarding cycles by the track.
Unlacing and tossing shoes
To free our sweltering feet,
Allowing the sand of millions then
To crowd between our toes.
We pushed heavily against its crumbling
Up the bank to clutch a weathered stake
And wobble as we crossed a leaning barbed wire fence.
Our cries and cackles carried
On the salty breeze
To join the curlews peet out on the strand.

And here where piled-up stones
Each nimbly perch against another
To enclose a crooked field
I turned my ankle, rolled a rock
And found down in the sheen of marram grass
A little stony heart.
And thought no more,
Until we found another
And knew at once it had been carefully sought out
And carried here
Cradled in her fingers as she marched behind
The tall men in dark suits who bore the box.
And in that moment, we felt lost and so alone.
And knew now that we were intruders here

Stumbling in an intimate spot
Where infant souls, deemed by doctrine
To be outcast, were taken to their rest.
Here where mothers come by night
To shed their sorrow on the breeze
To shut out dreams
To match their empty hollows to the sky
And dig their fingers down into the soil
To bind a moment to those innocents.
Safe here from all the world can do
They nestle where the rabbits thump along
Where skylarks soar to cast a blessing
And sand counts time forever.

One Adventure Yet

All along that black and buckled coast
They chased an ancient tongue
Clenched those clumsy vowels in their teeth
Caught them as they swept across the islands,
Plucked them from the breeze
And shook the life back into them,
Taught their tongues to turn and twist around the sound
And spit it right back in your face.
Released at last from obligation
Their generation's task complete,
Two sisters on the loose, they broke out the wine
Packed the rucksack, took the open road,
To stuff their cheeks with great gobs of Atlantic air
From tip of Lewis to Quimper
For years they could be found amongst the tunes
Or hunting out mass rocks,
Tracking Sheela-na-gigs in crumbling walls,
Caught in a squall in Donegal
Or nestled in a small white cottage further down the coast.
They were the hearty ones, with such a glow.
And though a single candle flame, in a cottage window frame
It seems like only yesterday
They gazed out from the cliff, across the ocean mist
And wondered if there was just time for one adventure yet.

Departed

They burdened us with ritual that autumn
Prayerful bedside vigils, candles, tea.
Then the funeral itself.
Familiar and restrained
Exposed that generation now stripped bare
Down to the last remaining prayer.
Beads, shriveled ancient berries from some distant season,
Entwined around cold fingers.
Grasping hard on memories.
Shoulders sunk in heavy coats
First bought when backs were broader,
A nephew's valediction
Met with absent concentration.
The duty of the coffin
Passed to another generation
'Who never knew us in our prime.'
A scuffle at the lift, as palms are clasped up on the backs of suited shoulders
Now steady footfalls echo back the years
As she is counted high, and proud
Step by step and row by row
Along the path of generations
Out to the open sky.

Crows call high from empty trees
While down to earth we stand erect
Stiffened by a clutch of firm hand grips
A muted last salute to a sister lost.
The final prayers are thinly broadcast to the breeze
And with one brief parting kiss of Irish rain
We catch the rattle and the spatter
Of hard soil spaded on to wood.
As the first car turns already on the road to Belfast. ⫽

Ghosts

Don't believe in ghosts? You ought!
In spite of what you have been taught.
For when you're coffined, buried, food
For worms or worse, you don't conclude.
We creatures aren't so easily wiped
Like some plastic card just swiped,
Our active era finished, ended,
In others heads we are extended.
For though we have ceased to exist,
In memories we will persist
Through any who recall our face
Or visit some familiar place
We're spoken of, recalled to mind
Resurrected, for a time.
Wherever friends or family meet
To mourn or christen, trick or treat
Summoned for the Christmas toast
An absent presence, familiar ghost.
Consulted when they have a drink
'If he were here, what would he think?'
Do not cry out with such alarm
'My reputation they will harm!'
The living seldom will, it's said
Ever speak ill of the dead.
And so, released from growing old
From ills and bills, bad news and cold
You'll carry on a further while
With still the power to raise a smile.

Fred

He would set out for north by first turning south,
Gravely scratch his head and knit his brow when asked the time,
Before commencing to address the question.
His passion was tradition cast aside
Re-kindled in the shaded afternoons around a pint
In that pub where older singers gather yet.
They patiently and silently observed
As he stood up and sang out verses by the dozen,
Neck out-stretched to try to make the pitch
Each word addressed with reverence and resolve,
His dog splayed wide around him on the floor.
He had it all inside his head, the knowledge and the scholarship,
Each song, its origin, the meanings we have lost.
He had old stories of the Ceili band,
World champions twice,
Of Woody Guthrie on the Liverpool waterfront,
Of how Cisco Houston came to Tithebarn Street
Bob Davenport at Gregson's Wells,
And where Paul Simon really sang in the company of strangers,
When no more than a boy.
He had a spotlight he could put on flummery
Was one of those who damned the rich
Called on comrades to stand up for justice and equality.
Upheld the virtues of flat caps and dribbling dogs.
Now he is gone, there are some songs
Will not be heard again. //

The Belfast Blitz

Fear ran rampant then
In the glances you encountered on the street
In your father's conversations
And in the eyes of strangers.

From the wireless in the living room
As you prepared for school each day
You overheard reports
And knew the life you'd been prepared for
Would soon be snatched away

And in that hour
There was no bugle call to arms for you.
You stepped up quietly, defiant of the danger
Your fragility encased in steel
Your good heart resolved
As you committed to what you knew by instinct must be done.

And when the terror was unleashed from the night time sky
As their relentless war machine
Thought you could be bombed into submission,
Indeed, they underestimated you, and all your kind.

You arose from dreams that night
Shocked back to reality by the blast,
The horizon of your future and your hopes
Instantly reduced from years to seconds.

In the smoke and flame, the blasted streets,
Your great coat flapped about you
Your squat standard issue helmet tipped at an angle
As you scrambled in the rubble of family homes,
Beside collapsing walls,
Clawing at the bricks, the broken furniture
To rescue children, grandparents, pets,
And heave dead bodies from the devastation.

Next morning over tea,
You dismissed all talk of bravery,
Wondering instead, how you'd ever get the stench of smoke out of your hair.

We never saw that side of you.
We saw you in your kitchen smock, in the dull 1950s
When you were thankful for a humdrum week
Of Monday wash and Friday fish.
Years later I came across it,
That rude helmet that once shielded your head
Now at the bottom of a wardrobe,
Along with fancy dress stuff
Green and bent,
Faded initials on the front
Redundant, in a house that never would be bombed.

In the Days Before They Left Iar Connaught for Chicago

This is loosely based on stories of the great Irish fiddle players of the 1920s. Iar means west.

In the days before they left Iar Connaught for Chicago
They would work on barns and cottages along the windy coast.
Day by day they measured up and spliced
Punched the steely spikes into the creamy wood
Casements, roofs and floors all conjured into shape.
And when it rained
Under shelter of the house
They would lay down their big claw hammers
Tenon saws and levels
To snap the hasps on fiddle cases,
Eager to pick up on Michael's twisty tunes.
Then the pencil which had earlier mapped joists
Was plucked out from behind an ear again
Gripped once more between the joiners stubby fingers
To rule out fine new lines upon the smooth white boards
And quickly sketch the busy zig-zag pattern of the dots.
'You see? It goes like this.'
So conjuring a tune upon the buttery wood
Fiddles crooked beneath their chins
They'd read and rattle out the melodies
Which escaped and sang across the barren fields and rocks,
Up to the ancient rookeries, and far across the quiet countryside.

And later back at work, fiddles locked away,
They'd measure up those pencilled beams
Slice through the tunes and firmly nail them in.
Melodies and memories of such music and such times
And such companionship
Locked into rafters, walls and attics
To bless the cottages along the windy coast
In the years before they left Iar Connaught for Chicago.

Two Uses for Cowhide

Jenny's chicken's is a stuttering and lively old Irish dance tune – enduringly popular and evocative. Geese in the Bog is another.

As forefinger and thumb adjust the silvery tubes by his side,
His elbow presses on the leather bag, hugging it tight,
To release the clucking and the cackle, Jenny's Chickens,
Strutting and skittering in the yard
Their squawking sharp as needles to the ear

And though the river is in spate,
He drops it lightly off his back,
And feeds the rounded boat on to the water
Tarred leather tight as goat hide on a drum
Glistening like seal skin, black as crow.
The coracle pitches, rucked against the wash,
Launching spume into the air
'Sure this thing is a law unto itself,' says the other.
'Ah,' says Michael, jerking back his head in that way that he does,
'I wouldn't part with her for millions.'
He grips the boat,
Feels the heartbeat of the river swell beneath his hand.
They move by signals long practiced,
Until there is a lull, then they are in,
Perched on half an acorn, in confident jeopardy,
Oars dipping to meet the frantic water, as they twirl again,
'They used to row to heaven in these things.'

Now he shuffles in his chair
Head lifted, tilted bird-like
Eyes to the distance
As if the notes were written on the sky.
Fingers settle on the chanter,
Those unruly notes,
Geese in the bog
They scatter honking here and there,
Until he rounds them up, one by one,
Ordering the sound, slowly rising to a melody,
A new landscape revealed

Coming from the long-time past
Vaulting forward, Jenny's Chickens,
Reeling in the light. ∥

Gone to Canada

In those days she still had her flat
And a part-time job in Asda
Which was not far from the library.
And sometimes after work
She'd walk over to the library
Where she'd open up the atlas of the world,
To find the map of Canada,
Which was where they said her mother went.
And then one day Ann McMullan from the library showed her
Where you'd find all the other books on Canada.

And so she found the legend of the chieftain Hiawatha
And the slaying of the great bear of the mountains, Mishe-Mokwa,
And the story of the Morning Star and Princess Minihaha
On the shores of mighty Huron, in the land of Laughing Water.

He was sleeping out, when they referred him to the hostel
Where he got a small room on his own, up on the second floor,
And he went to the meeting every week, so they could decide his programme.
They sent him to the library, 'A key component for your folder,' Brian said,
And that was where they met, when he needed help with logging on
And she showed him what to do, and they began to talk.
And that became something for them both to look forward to each Wednesday
And sometimes, when she'd finished shelving books
Ann McMullan made them both a cup of tea,

And they read about the legend of the chieftain Hiawatha
And the slaying of the great bear of the mountains, Mishe-Mokwa,
And the story of the Morning Star and Princess Minihaha
On the shores of mighty Huron, in the land of Laughing Water.

Then things began to change, and rents went up
So she had to leave her flat, and go sleeping at her sister's,
Where they didn't have the room, but wouldn't see her on the streets.

And he was OK for a time,
After Brian found a place for him to move to from the hostel
Until they cut his money and he had to move again.
But they still kept in touch each Wednesday at the library,
Where they would sit and talk on the bench outside
And they even gave out leaflets at the time of the campaign,
But in the end the library was closed,
And Ann McMullan had to go and get some other job.

Now on the busy days when she can't go to the flat
Because her sister is still there with all the kids

She goes over to the library, if it's dry,
To sit down on the bench,
Where they all sit out in the afternoon.
And she looks in through the window where all the books are kept locked up
And dream that they might open it again one day,
And then he might come back,
And Ann McMullan might make them both a cup of tea,

And they might return once more to the land of Hiawatha
And read about the slaying of the Great Bear, Mishe-Mokwa,
And all about the Morning Star and Princess Minihaha
On the shores of mighty Huron, in the land of Laughing Water

In Canada, where they say her mother went.

The Rules of War

From an original idea of Tony Murphy's, Liverpool poet and song writer.

You can use a Gatling gun, to kill the soldiers in their ranks
Armalites, Kalashnikovs, Hawker Hunters, Chieftain tanks,
You can use a long range rifle, a garrotte or poison dart,
You can take a twelve inch bayonet and run it through his heart.
You can burn him in his bunker, or shoot him up the ass
But for God's sake, chaps, be reasonable, don't go using gas.

You can pound him with artillery, from a health-n-safety distance
You can mow him down in hundreds, with machine guns in an instance
If you catch him as a spy, you have the right to execute him
Or if you are old fashioned, just yank out a gun and shoot him.
You can hand grenade him, cannonade him, but my friends, alas,
The one thing that you cannot do is use that nasty gas.

You can blindfold and abduct him, and chuck him on a plane
Fly him half way round the world til he's never seen again
Zip him in a jump suit, shackle him in chains
Water board and beat him 'til he's nearly lost his brains,
You can lock him up behind barbed wire, stone walls and toughened glass,
But whatever you decide on, just ensure you don't use gas.

You can drop an H-bomb or an A-bomb and incinerate his town
Devastate the country for a hundred miles around
Blow the whole damn world to bits in a nuclear war,
You might as well, why not, that's what the things are for
That nuclear high technology is such a touch of class
Far more sophisticated (don't you think) than dirty low down gas.

Ramadan

Close to midnight
I was waiting in the dark, engine running,
When they burst out from the yellow pool of light
And clustered, in the narrow street.
Distant figures, I could just make out
Marching now intently towards the car.
Shadows flitting in the headlights
Bearded urgent men, clad in black,
Each face intent as they advanced,
Brushing against the wing mirrors
In their hurry from the back-street mosque

Faith of their fathers, living still,
Rooted under northern skies,
The glories of a distant past in their minds,
Certainties to hold in times of siege
Fables in an ancient tongue
Customs of the desert
Adapted to another place and time.

And now they hurry home
Not plotting devastation,
But intent on breaking fast,
Getting off to bed
To rise again at dawn:

Another day of fasting,
Of children off to school
Of work
Of prayers.

Seeds

He cradled them securely in his hand
To fix them in his mind
Before committing them to soil.
On such as these were empires built.

The cage around his memories
Held fast the faces from his youth
Lest they too take flight
To leave behind but echoes
In the lonely chambers of his heart.

In this country of tarmac and concrete
Where they do not grow or harvest
He paced the rain-swept streets
In his search for soil.

He found this damaged acre,
Hemmed around by brickwork
Neglected home to vagrants like himself,
The ginger fox, blue butterflies and feral pigeons.

Amid the rubble and the plastic
His hands called up the skills of generations
Unlocked again the dormant force of life beneath
Allowed the seeds of Africa
To root in foreign ground.
Mustard, purple borage, lufa,
Spear grass of the Stipea tribe.
Thirsty for the tantalising taste of life
Breathing in the Toxteth air.
And did they like him have recall of the desert heat,
The haik, and the scent of camel?

The Fiery Couch

Maybe it's because she lives alone now
Talking loudly as she wanders the house
Worrying the curtains and the cushions
Getting angry at the faces on the screen
Who ignore her when she rants.
And when that's run its course,
She turns to the old stories
Reciting her familiar monologues
To keep the conversation going
Recounting one by one
As if for the first time
The anthems of her years
The random milestones of a life
Bound up in family.
Flotsam of a generation,
Risen to the surface
Floating in a memory lock
As they turn and turn.

'You were just a babe in arms
When your father jumped off the pier at Carrick
And disappeared below the water.
How we laughed as you cried your eyes out
Until he popped up again.'
'Did I ever tell you that your aunty Sheila once set the couch on fire
Falling asleep with a cigarette in her hand
Such thick black smoke
And all her life savings in it?'
'And you should never go down the Grand Canyon.
Your uncle Frankie did
That year when they went out to the States
To see Danny.
And then he couldn't climb back up again.
They had to fetch a buggy just to get him out.'
'And do you remember Bernie's wee dog.
Hit by a car.
And when the police brought him back

We all thought someone had died.
But it was just the wee dog coming back.'

And when I call at weekends
It all comes pouring out
I know each one by heart now,
So that when she goes
Those old chapters of our family,
Dad's epic dive, Bernie's wee dog
Frankie in the Grand Canyon, Sheila's fiery couch
Will live on a little longer
In my head.

Vanished

In Silvester Street in Liverpool there is a small children's playground which was formerly a graveyard in which many of those fleeing the Irish Famine were buried in the 1840s. Their remains have since been removed.

Weathered sandstone pillars mark the threshold,
Exhausted ground of tarmac, stone and railing,
Sweet soil, that once gave birth to daffodils and snowdrops
Now trampled underfoot and barren
You hold on our behalf the burdens of the past,
Last relics of the vanished people
Whose voice was ever drowned

Is there prospect of redemption here?
Should I stretch out upon this ground,
To weep my tears into the soil?
To claw the senseless earth
Conjure it to life and claim it back?

More bone than flesh
You came to rest here in the heart of Vauxhall;
The tarmac and the stunted grass cannot remember
That you once had dreams of the wild Atlantic crossing,
You whose bones now tremble by the waterfront
To the rhythm of the lorries' rumble.

Here dignity in death was the kindness of strangers.
The grandeur of the church not granted,
The sky became your vaulted canopy
The salty mist your unction
The merciful dark your coffin.
Who was it passed you down,
In threadbare winding sheet, by single candle-light,
Their solemn prayers whispered to the wind?

Do lingering bones still cower here
Like the jagged ribs of some old shipwreck?
Are there skulls, each an empty tabernacle
That once cradled memories and dreams?

Handkerchief

By firelight in the quiet stretch of long Ulster winter evenings
Stitch by stitch she drove the needle point into the fabric she had chosen
To weave the pattern of the name she'd given him
And so bestow her blessing,
With hopes for his safe passage.

He took it without ceremony, secret in his pocket.
Symbol of the bond between them.
And in the lonely nights, behind dull seminary walls
He held it fast,
Protected from the gaze of those who'd mock such sentimental relics,
And desecrate the fragile thread that linked them heart to heart.

For years that modest gift fulfilled its mundane purpose
Until that day the brutal gunfire from troops
Unleashed sudden death into the unsuspecting crowd
Extinguishing the fragile pulse of life on every side.
There along the narrow streets
Bloodstained it fluttered in his hand, as he maintained his steady progress
Crouching by the edge of death,
The injured cradled in the arms of those behind him
A piteous shield,
Exposed to the rude gaze of all the world, he held it high,
Her embroidery between his fingers,
Symbol of the bond between them
And her hopes for his safe passage.

Why Ferry Turf by Boat?
The annual Crinniu Na mBad festival celebrates the arrival in Kinvara of turf from across Galway Bay, carried in traditional boats, as has been the custom for centuries. The journey around the bay by lorry is much faster, more convenient and more logical. 'Bad' (pronounced bawd) is the Irish word for boat.

The lorry driver in his cab
Never has the need
Ahead of setting out
To feel the wind direction and its speed,
To shade his forehead with a calloused hand
To look about the sky with weathered eye
To scan the far horizon.
Never needs to know the detail
Of the rocks and tides
To ever urgently duck under
A rotating spar
Is never caught out listing in a gust
Never drops his hand to touch cold water
As the sleek black heavy *bad* beneath
Of timber and traditioned tackle
Leans to and slices through, driving foam ahead
With no sound but the flapping of red canvas.
Never wipes a salty spit
Plucked and flung by an unruly breeze
Will never suck the tang of turf and seaweed in
Or lose his cap
Never roll a rise of water
Never needs to eye approaching moorings,
Calculating all at once the wind, the tide
The moment of the boat
When – locked at one with it – he shifts the rudder just a touch.
Never catches sight of wheeling gulls
As he stumbles out to grab and bring down
Sails ballooned in chaos.
Never flings a heavy length of rope
And thuds it to a chest.
Never has the need of twenty hands
To toss each sod of turf
On to the cobbled pier
At the far end of the day.

Rostrevor

Rostrevor is a seaside town in County Down, popular with caravaners.

We met at the camp site down by Rostrevor.
I asked for a kiss, and she said 'Never.'
The girls on the campsite were all Dolly Partons,
But she was in blue jeans, and yellow Doc Martins.

I bought her an ice cream, but she wouldn't lick it
I bought her a rose bud, she told me to stick it
Her hair was so curly, I told her I liked it,
Next day she chopped it, greased it and spiked it.

I said what you drinkin, she said gin with a chaser
She gave me the push when I tried to embrace her.
We talked about music and I tried to bluff it
When I said Paul Simon, she told me to stuff it.

We went to the pictures, sat in the back row
She said you're more ugly than Robert De Niro.
I said that I thought I resembled George Clooney
She said to be honest you're more like Wayne Rooney

I gave her a shamrock, she rolled it and smoked it,
I made her a promise and she went and broke it.
Her hairstyle was punk, her face new romantic,
Her jacket was Goth, her mother was frantic.

At the Halloween dance I was Conan the Barbarian,
She said you'd be scarier dressed as a librarian.
I said, 'I'm Catholic', she said, 'I'm pagan',
I said, 'I like burgers', she said 'I'm Vegan.'

Her sister was Vuitton, her scarf was Versace
She was more Oxfam, her hair was Apache.
When we met her family, I was shocked to discover
She had a conventional father and brother

I wore a white shirt, a tie and a blazer,
She was in ripped tights, a chain and a razor.
I walked her home, my arm on her shoulder,
I asked for a kiss, but she said, 'When you're older.'

I told her 'I love you', she said, 'Whatever.'
She said, 'For how long.' I said, 'Forever.'

Each Time You Kill a Tree

You kill more than ten thousand times
Each time you kill a tree.
For trees can live a hundred years
And every year ten thousand leaves
To curtain over ground
And every leaf in turn a world
For maggots, moths and mites
A hold a home a larder
Of sap and shade and shelter
Where spiders spin and crickets sing
Where birds may feed, and make their home
And hatch their young
Who will in turn,
Endow this world with song.

And when trees blossom in the spring,
Then butterflies and wasps and bees
Will suck that rich dark nectar which
Is found unique in trees
And flowers in turn will run to seed
And seeds will sow in soil
To yield a thousand trees

Yes, you kill more than ten thousand times
Each time you kill a tree
For trees can live hundreds of years
And make ten thousand seeds.

Fulmar

There must be cliffs
And there must be breaking waves against them.
There must be open sky with all its promise
There must be restless wind,
Which summons us to wander.

Do not talk to me of woods and meadows,
Of quiet afternoons down in the grass,
There must be water, white foam kicked up
Water, where you can jet down from the air
To crash out of one world into another
Where the ocean tightly folds around you
Where sounds are muted into dreamscapes
Where you can hunt and press the silver flesh of fish

What was it that gifted us such feathers,
That we can push and rise, shake free again of water
Beat hard against the air,
Stretch and beat,
Upwards yet, back to the open sky
To be again forever, riders on the wind?

Grass

What is it about grass?
Why can't it just leave us alone?
Why can't it find its own bloody place and stay away.
Why must it try to cover, well, everything.
No, really,
Why must it insist that, in the end, 'The earth is mine'?
When in fact, we are humankind, the earth is ours.
Look grass: We have won. Get over it.
But no. Bloody stubborn grass. Just can't accept defeat.
We have invented concrete, tarmac, motorways, built New York,
But even in the cities you will find bloody stubborn grass.

You will find the evil stuff,
All consuming, empire building,
Always in the places where it shouldn't be.
We have been misled, misguided,
Thinking we can tame it, trim it, mow it down.
Turf and sod it, cut it
Paint white lines along it
Trample it with studded boots.
But mutinous, ungrateful, acquisitive grass
Will not remain cowed for long.
No matter how we maltreat it,
Plough it, poison it,
Breed a million cattle sheep and goats to eat it
Grass never sleeps or takes a holiday.

You might think that as a city dweller you are safe from grass,
Inside of some glossy office block
Shielded by unyielding concrete, yards of polished glass, perfect tarmac
Miles from any field or park.
But haven't you noticed, take a look
Between the pebbles on the gravel, in the gutters,
Around the paving stones, in the very turrets of the roof,
Grass…..watching, waiting.
'Our day will come.'
Its stated policy and programme

To win back every inch,
To a make a glorious grassy empire of the earth,
To cover and destroy each trace of us
To bury every one of us beneath its treacherous root.
As if we'd never been.
Whatever happens, we may rule today
But just remember this.
Grass abides.
Do not bank on it surrendering any time soon.

Zero Emissions

Gears and grips
Guards and gadgets
Brackets, brakes, ball bearings,
Panniers, pedals, pump,
Post and pinion,
Links, lugs, levers, lights,
Cogs, caps and cable,
Crank, and chain,
Greased and geared,
Wheel rims,
Saddle, spokes, and springs
Frame and fork,
Tested tubes and tyres,
Bonded, buckled, burnished,
Bike. //

Her Chair

The empty seat was there
When we next sat down
To share the spoken word
And was there again
When we gathered at West Kirby in the summer.
Or at the pavement tables by the Phil in autumn.
Eloquently silent,
It carried on its melancholy dialogue with each of us in turn.
Listening to what we had to say
As we addressed it from the mike.
And as we rose to go that night, how cold it seemed,
That empty chair that once had been the warmest.

Then afterwards it followed me
Four stiff legs rocking awkwardly along the pavement
Trying to keep up,
A lost puppy, latching on to one who had made eye contact
Refusing to be shaken off.
And often in a café, or some crowded place in town
Against the rise of voices in the bookshop,
I can hear its distinctive clip and clop
Just behind me.

Down in These Waters

Down in these waters
Who knows how many keys have come to rest,
Each one a witness to a vow
A secret,
To which two hearts alone can testify
Yet neither can retrieve.
Here each one takes its place amongst a thousand others
Those carelessly tossed, as scraps cast to the dogs
Those tender as a valentine in satin
Committed to the waves.
All derelict as shipwrecks now
They lie against the granite quay-stones
While above them at the water's edge
The city sets its weathered face
Westward to the wind
And every traveller knows
From this point on
You must commit your fortune to the ocean
Your promise to the caprice of the winds.

Sue

She settled in that part of town
That lies beneath the gaze of Georgian windows,
Where car tyres rumble hard along the cobble stones.
Marking her territory with window boxes,
Runner beans and hanging baskets.
In varnished nails and gardening boots
She wove her silky web around our lives.

Evergreen as ivy
She was of the breed
That overwintered by warm firesides
And put down roots in the fertile soil
Of good companions.
Of sunny aspect, she preferred a sheltered spot
And would blossom in the warmth of lasting friendship
And in the company of children.

Favouring sunlight over shade,
Elegant and willowy
She was nonetheless of hardy stock,
Which could withstand inclement weather
And resist those thorns and weeds
Which seek to undermine the common good.

She nurtured one and all
Cascading white and blue lobelia
The ruffled blossoms of petunia
Infernos of begonia
To brighten Faulkner Street.

Delicate as eyebright was her open smile
The light blue bells of Canterbury her laugh.
She was wild as garlic, steady as the oak,
Flamed montbretia, and the yellow clad archangel
All in one.

Apple Blossom

It was as if they knew it was to be their final season
For they were rampant, rank on rank,
Blossom upon apple blossom, crowding towards the light,
Mountainous and fragile, oozing life.
Breathing their sweet fragrance to the earth.

Here every creature of the trees might find a home,
Dewdrops caught the light of dawn
Where they hung suspended from those nets that spiders spin
Lady birds would light and flip their wings
And in the height of summer
Butterflies would stagger leaf to leaf
While swallows swooped so recklessly above

The heavy air was loud with bees
Drunk on the aroma, their dizzied flight
Returning and returning
To burrow in the blossom
Harvesting day long.

Not anymore.
Fallen to the anger of the petrol driven chainsaw
The dead limbs sundered in a moment,
Sliced and carried off ingloriously,
In crass humiliation, to the waiting skip.

Do bees remember and return
To that same spot time and again
To dream of the aroma and the heat,
To seek the soft satin of the petals
To search out the sticky rich intoxication of the nectar?

While somewhere far away in a waste disposal site
Dead limbs are rotting
And along with them the secret ancient formula
For creating apple blossom.

Arenig Fawr

Arenig Fawr is a mountain in north Wales where, in 1911-12, James Dickson Innes and Augustus John created a series of outstanding landscape paintings. In the same area, in 1943, a United States flying fortress bomber crashed, killing all on board.

The wind was snapping hard about
As we rose to higher ground
The steady rhythm of centuries
Was drumming on our cheeks
Beating down the heather
And pounding flat circles on the grass.
It carries not a shred of memory
Anniversaries all forgot:
The past as empty as the future.

We caught our breath where they once stood
Those who first carved a living from these lofty open hills
And fought dogged to defend them.

On such a scattered day, a century past
They sat hereabouts, John and Innes
To look down these same distances
And seek pinks, purples and deep blues
-- where I see only dun and brown –
To conjure warmth and colour,
When I can only draw my coat more tightly.

And driving home in dark
I cannot help but think again
On those who struck the monolith that night
To be counted now amongst the not returned
So hearty in their faded photograph
Those boys in bomber jackets, of Michigan, New York and Florida.

My mind still wind-whipped
Drops of cloud still glistening in my hair
I promise to return
To the silence of your histories,
Arenig Fawr.

Iron Man
On Anthony Gormley's Other Place sculptures, Crosby Beach, Lancashire.

Here where oyster-catchers flit along the empty stretch,
Resolute you face into the pathway of the setting sun
Escorting it to earth each dusk,
Watchful through the night,
As you wait its warming touch upon your back
When once more it lights the shimmering miles of sand and sea.

Under open skies you silently submit
To the waxing of the moon, the flowing tides,
Impassive when assaulted by the anger of the storm,
You hum instead an eerie canticle to the wind.
Though placid, dark and solitary,
You had a frenzied origin,
Hewed from fractured earth, forged by hand and fire,
To be anchored here in sand.
Do you now count the grains
To measure out the depth of time?
Do you observe the passage of the ships,
And mark them one by one as they approach the port,
Sending ripples to the shore
To tremble at your feet
And summon up a dream
That you might one day rouse your heavy limbs
To stiffly wade into the waves, board ship
And set off to discover what it is that lies beyond the tantalising far horizon?

I found you cold at first,
Yet in time I came to understand your constancy.
While sands shift, tides ruck and roll around you, people gather and depart,
You keep your watch at the entrance to the city
Dedicated to your duty,
A model for this distracted age.

The purpose of your vigil not revealed
In that determined stance, and stolid enigmatic face
Each of us must then divine the purpose,
And draw some slow profound reply
Resounding from that mighty iron heart
Once hewed from fractured earth, forged by hand and fire
To stand alone along the shore,
Attuned by night and day to transmissions of the wind
The water and the firmament.
Here you whistle to the wilderness,
Bear witness to the change,
Become a muted harbinger
Of the fast approaching storm.

Snowflake

You cannot put a bar code on a snowflake,
It doesn't matter who you think you are.
You cannot set a boundary to a dream
Or put a price-tag on a shooting star.

You can't take an idea out and shoot it
Or lock it up behind prison bars.

You can't arrest a poem and execute it
Or crush it with a fleet of armoured cars.

You'd like to hoover up ideas
Parcel up and ticket all the dreams
Wrap them tight in cellophane and plastic
Pump them out in bulk from slot machines.

You'd like to put a patent on to birdsong
And charge us when a robin sings a tune
You'd like to send an invoice to the mother
Each time her child gazes at the moon.

You are attracted to the notion
To designate each hillside corporate land;
You'd love to privatise the ocean
Charge us for each walk along the strand.

But you cannot make a sandwich from a dollar,
Goose liver paté out of gold;
Cannot eat the money that you've made
When all the world is bought and sold.

You cannot trap kindness in a bottle
Put it on a supermarket shelf.
Or open up a tin of happiness
Every time you want to help yourself.

You cannot put a use-by date on friendship
And stash it in the freezer next the peas
With a message to 'defrost before using'
This is an item that you can't refreeze.

You can fool some of the people with mass media
From Amsterdam to Boston via… Bulgaria
But there'll always be some tosser who will cheat ya
With unexpected items in the blagging area.

You cannot put a barcode on a snowflake
It doesn't matter who you think you are
You cannot set a boundary to our dreams
Or put a price-tag on a shooting star.

Other anthologies and collections available from Stairwell Books

The Exhibitionists	Ed. Rose Drew and Alan Gillott
The Green Man Awakes	Ed. Rose Drew
Fosdyke and Me and Other Poems	John Gilham
Along the Iron Veins	Ed. Alan Gillott and Rose Drew
Gringo on the Chickenbus	Tim Ellis
Running with Butterflies	John Walford
Late Flowering	Michael Hildred
Scenes from the Seedy Underbelly of Suburbia	Jackie Simmons
Pressed by Unseen Feet	Ed. Rose Drew and Alan Gillott
York in Poetry Artwork and Photographs	Ed. John Coopey and Sally Guthrie
Taking the Long Way Home	Steve Nash
Skydive	Andrew Brown
Still Life With Wine and Cheese	Ed. Rose Drew and Alan Gillott
Somewhere Else	Don Walls
Sometimes I Fly	Tim Goldthorpe
49	Paul Lingaard
Homeless	Ed. Ross Raisin
The Ordinariness of Parrots	Amina Alyal
New Crops from Old Fields	Ed. Oz Hardwick
Throwing Mother in the Skip	William Thirsk-Gaskill
The Problem with Beauty	Tanya Nightingale
Learning to Breathe	John Gilham
Unsettled Accounts	Tony Lucas
Lodestone	Hannah Stone
The Beggars of York	Don Walls
Rhinoceros	Daniel Richardson
More Exhibitionism	Ed. Glen Taylor
Heading for the Hills	Gillian Byrom-Smith
Nothing Is Meant to be Broken	Mark Connors
Northern Lights	Harry Gallagher
Poetry for the Newly Single 40 Something	Maria Stephenson
Gooseberries	Val Horner
A Thing of Beauty Is a Joy Forever	Don Walls
The River Was a God	David Lee Morgan
The Glass King	Gary Allen
Something I Need to Tell You	William Thirsk-Gaskill
Where the Hares Are	John Gilham
Steel Tipped Snowflakes 1	Izzy Rhiannon Jones, Becca Miles, Laura Voivodeship
Blue Saxophone	Rosemary Palmeira

For further information please contact rose@stairwellbooks.com
www.stairwellbooks.co.uk
@stairwellbooks